— God's Creation Ser

WTHE
ORLD
GOD MADE

Edward J. Shewan

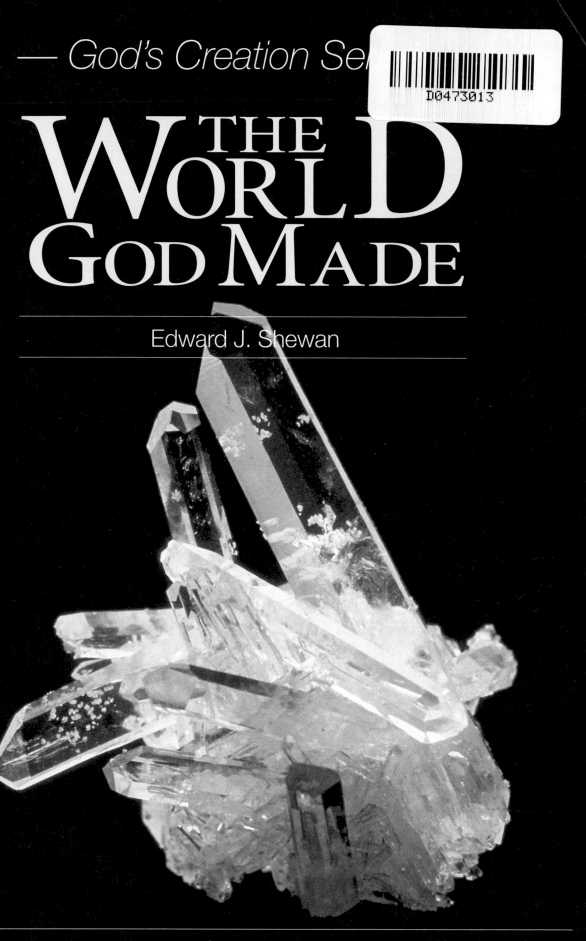

RISTIAN LIBERTY PRESS

CHRISTIAN LIBERTY PRESS
502 W. Euclid Avenue
Arlington Heights, IL 60004

www.homeschools.org

Christian Liberty Press

502 W. Euclid Avenue
Arlington Heights, IL 60004

www.homeschools.org

Scripture References are conformed to the Holy Bible, New King James Version ©1982, Thomas Nelson, Inc., so that modern readers may gain greater comprehension of the Word of God.

Author: Edward J. Shewan
General Editorship: Michael J. McHugh
Designer: Robert Fine
Photography: Digital Stock, Robert Fine, James E. Dau, Corel, Artville, Photo Disc
Graphics: Christopher Kou, Edward J. Shewan
Cover Photo: Robert Fine

Printed in the United States of America

ISBN 1-930367-00-7

— Contents —

— Preface —

Young students need to learn how God made the earth and heavens in six days. The book that follows will help children to better understand that the things that they observe in creation were made by God alone.

When young people study *The World God Made*, they will discover how often nature sings of the majesty and power of the Creator, God the Father. The works of creation continually testify to the greatness of the Lord and inspire true students of science to explore the world with diligence.

The Bible reminds each creature that the fear of the Lord is the beginning of all true knowledge. In this regard, it is vital that young students acknowledge the work of their Creator as they seek to gain a knowledge of the world around them. Great joy and wisdom will flow to all those who are committed to glorifying Christ through a study of the created order.

Michael J. McHugh
Arlington Heights, IL
2000

DAY 1
The Heavens and the Earth

*In
the
beginning*

*God created the heavens
and the earth.*
Genesis 1:1

God Created the Heavens and the Earth

The first verse in the Bible tells us, "In the beginning God created the heavens and the earth." This means that there is "one God and Father of all" (Ephesians 4:6) who created everything.

God created everything in six days. The first chapter of the Bible tells us what He made on each day of creation. This book will teach you many things about what God made on these six days.

How Did God Create the Heavens and the Earth?

By faith we understand that the worlds were framed by the word of God, so that the things which are seen were not made of things which are visible. Hebrews 11:3

The Lord spoke and created everything in the heavens and the earth. He made the worlds out of **nothing**. Can you make something from nothing? No, you need paper and crayons to make a picture. You need paint and a brush to make a painting.

The Bible tells us that God made the worlds only by His word. He created the heavens and the earth out of nothing. And He did all of this in six days! This is why God alone is the great Creator.

Draw or paint a picture in the picture frame below.

What Was the Earth Like?

The earth was without form. Genesis 1:2a

NO SHAPE

The Bible tells us the earth was **"without form."** This means the earth had no shape. Can you think of something that does not have shape? Water is something that does not have shape.

Activity

Fill a jar with water. The water takes the shape of the jar. If you pour the jar of water into a bowl, it takes the shape of the bowl. Try filling other things that have different shapes. What does the water do?

The earth was like water that was not put into a jar or bowl. It was only floating in space. Because the water was not put into something, it was like a blob of water floating in the heavens.

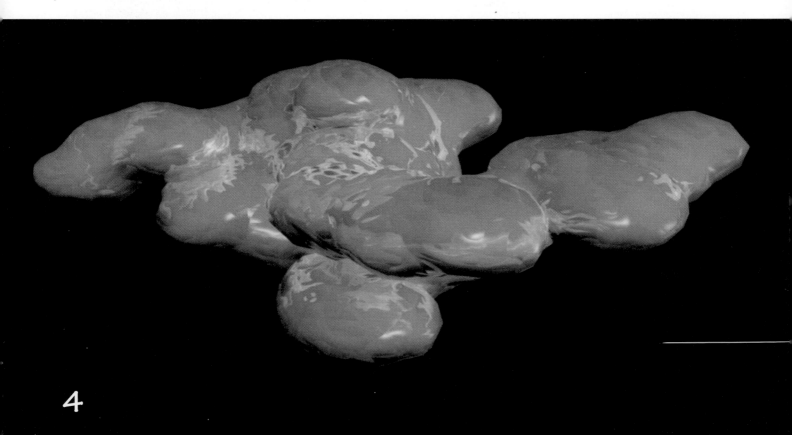

Something To Color:
What is the earth like now?

Color the picture of the earth below. This is what it looks like now—a ball that is covered with land and water. *Color the water blue and the land green or brown.*

Who Gave Life to the Earth?

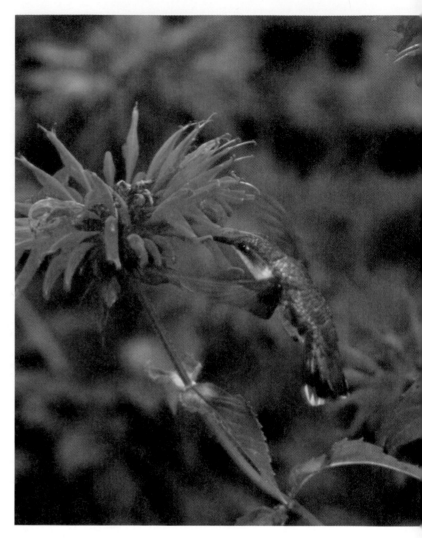

And the Spirit of God was hovering over the face of the waters. Genesis 1:2 b

The Bible tells us that the Spirit of God was **"hovering"** over the top of the waters. Hovering means to move slowly over something like a hummingbird hovers over a flower. This is how the Spirit of God brought life to the earth.

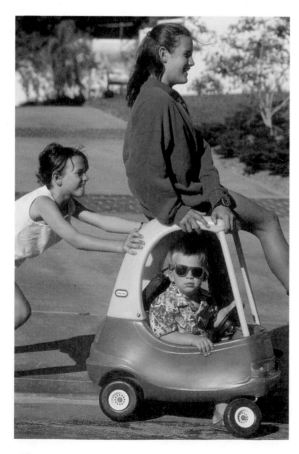

The Spirit of God brought life to all of creation. 2 Corinthians 3:6 says that the Spirit gives life. He helps you to live and work. The Spirit also helps you run, jump, and play.

God Created *Light*

Then God said, "Let there be light"; and there was light. Genesis 1:3

On Day One, God created light. Why do you think God made the light? He created the light so that we can see.

God created the light, and the darkness disappeared. Did God make the sun on the first day of creation? No, but He did create light. Without light we cannot see at all.

The Bible teaches that God is light (1 John 1:5b). God not only created light, but He is the Light of the world (John 1:9, 8:12).

Jesus Is the Light of the World

> Then Jesus spoke
> to them again, saying,
> "I am the light of the world.
> He who follows Me shall not
> walk in darkness, but have
> the light of life."
> John 8:12

People who do not know Jesus live in darkness. They cannot see in the darkness because of their sin. They need Jesus to lead them.

Jesus came to free His children from the power of sin and death. Jesus destroyed the power of darkness by dying on the cross to pay for the sins of His people. When God's children believe the good news of Christ's perfect life, death, and resurrection, they become new creations (2 Corinthians 5:17).

If you trust in Christ, you will also become a new creation (Ephesians 2:8-9). If you confess your sins and believe that Jesus died and rose again, you will be saved (Acts 2:38).

Light and Darkness

God divided the light from the darkness. Genesis 1:4b

When God created light, He **divided** the darkness from the light. God called the light "Day," and the darkness "Night."

God knew we needed the light in the daytime to do our work. He also knew we needed the darkness in the nighttime so we could rest. Did you know that children need at least eight hours of sleep each night?

Something to Color:

What do you do during the day? What do you do at night? ***Color the pictures.***

Looking Back

Questions

1. Who created the heavens and the earth?
2. How did God create the world?
3. Who gave life to the world?
4. How many days did God take to create everything?
5. What was the earth like in the beginning?
6. Why did God create the light?
7. How much sleep do children need each night?

Fill in the blank

1. _____ created the heavens and the earth.
2. The _____ of God hovered over the face of the waters.
3. Then God said, "Let there be _____ "; and there was light.
4. God called the light _____.
5. God called the darkness _____.
6. _____ is the Light of the world.

DAY 2
The Sky

Then God said, "Let there be a firmament in the midst of the waters, and let it divide the waters from the waters." Genesis 1:6

What is the Sky?

God made the firmament. Genesis 1:7a

On Day Two, God made the earth ready for plants, animals, and people to live. He decided to make something very helpful for all living things. God made the **firmament**.

WHAT IS THE FIRMAMENT?

This big word means the "sky." The sky is very important for all living things. The sky is filled with air. Without air, all the plants, animals, and people on Earth would die. All living things need to breathe and grow.

"Waters Above"

Firmament or Sky

"Waters Below"

God Divided the Waters

Then God said, "Let there be a firmament in the midst of the waters, and let it divide the waters from the waters." Genesis 1:6

God **divided** the waters which covered the earth. He placed the sky between the "waters above" and the "waters below."

God formed the earth into a ball covered with water. This was called, "the waters below."

God covered the earth with a layer called the "firmament" or sky. It was filled with air. This is what you breathe when you take in a breath.

Take a deep breath. You just breathed in some air!

Then God made another layer of water that covered the sky and the earth. This layer is called "the waters above." It was clear. Do you know what it was filled with? It was filled with water vapor.

What Is Water?

Water is a liquid that you drink every day. Water has no color and it is clear. God filled the earth with water from the very first day of creation. Water is a special gift that God has given to all living things.

How much do you weigh? More than half of your body weight is made up of water. We need to drink lots of water every day. If you stop drinking water for one week, you would become very sick.

Activity

Water

Fill a glass with some water. If you tip the glass a little bit the liquid moves with the glass. Water has no shape of its own. Water takes the shape of the thing that holds it. Drink some of the water.

Ice

Pour some water into an ice cube tray. Put the tray in the freezer overnight. What happened to the water? It became cold and hard. The water is no longer a liquid. It has turned into a solid called ice.

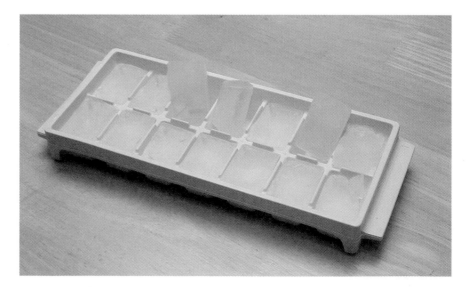

What Is Water Vapor?

Water vapor is like the steam from a teakettle. When you boil water, it seems to disappear. Where does it go? It becomes a gas and floats into the air.

A **gas** is something that has no shape and floats in space. This is what the "waters above" were like. They protected all living things from harmful beams of sunlight; these beams may burn the skin.

Activity

With the help of your teacher, boil water in a teakettle or pot. What happens to the water? It turns into steam that has no shape and floats in the air. The water becomes steam or water vapor.

God Created the Clouds

After the great Flood, God filled the sky with all kinds of clouds. They are made up of water droplets or tiny bits of ice that float above the earth. Clouds show us the glory of God.

WHAT DO CLOUDS LOOK LIKE?

Have you seen a cloud that looks like the one in this picture? God made many different kinds of clouds. Some are curly. Others are puffy. Still others are like cotton balls.

Activity

You will need a piece of paper, cotton, and glue to do this activity.

Divide the piece of paper into three parts. In the first part, glue cotton in the shape of curls. Glue cotton in the shape of puffy clouds in the second part. Then glue cotton in the shape of cotton balls in the third part.

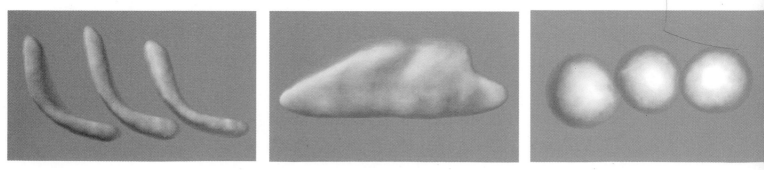

Rain and Snow

GOD MADE THE RAIN

Rain comes from water vapor in the sky. When the water vapor gets cooler, it forms drops of water. These drops of water fall to the ground as rain.

Do you know why we need the rain? The rain gives people, animals, and plants fresh water to drink.

GOD MADE THE SNOW

Snow is also made from water vapor, but this vapor never becomes drops of water like rain does. When this vapor becomes very cold, it quickly changes into tiny pieces of ice.

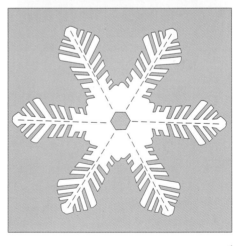

These tiny pieces of ice form snowflakes. Did you know that God makes each snowflake different? God also gives each snowflake six sides.

Something To Do:
Paper Snowflakes

Take a square piece of paper and draw a circle (using a bowl or cup) on the paper. Cut out the circle, fold it in half, then fold it in thirds. Cut a deep "V" shape on the round part. On the folded sides, cut different shapes. Now open your snowflake!

Looking Back

Questions

1. What is another name for the firmament?
2. Why did God create the sky?
3. What is water?

Matching

firmament   steam

water vapor   drops of water

rain   sky

Fill in the blank

1. Water vapor is like _Steam_ from a teakettle.

2. God filled the firmament or sky with _Clouds_.

3. A _rain_ is made up of water droplets or tiny bits of ice that float above the earth.

4. The _rain_ gives people, animals, and plants fresh water to drink.

5. A gas is something that has no shape and floats in _air_.

DAY 3
The Dry Land, Seas, and Plants

Then God said, "Let the waters under the heavens be gathered together into one place, and let the dry land appear"; and it was so. Genesis 1:9

God Created the Dry Land

Then God said, "Let the waters under the heavens be gathered together into one place, and let the dry land appear"; and it was so. Genesis 1:9

What did God **divide** on Day One of creation? God divided the light from the darkness. What did God divide on Day Two? God divided the waters—the waters above and the waters below.

On Day Three, God divided something else. He divided the land from the seas. God said, "Let the waters under the heavens be gathered together into one place, and let the dry land appear." God called the dry land "Earth" and the gathered waters "Seas."

Color the picture of the land and water. What color is the land? (tan or brown) What color is the water? (Blue)

Why Did God Create the Dry Land?

If God had not made the dry land, you would have no place to walk or play or live. He also made the dry land so all the land animals and plants could live and grow. God is wise in what He does.

Plant

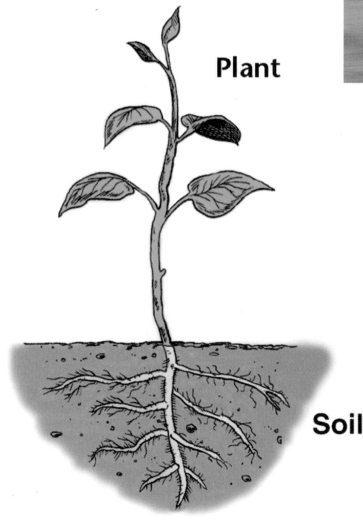

Soil

God created all kinds of dry land—soil, sand, and rocks.

Soil is good because it helps plants to grow.

God Created the Seas

The gathering together of the waters He called Seas.
Genesis 1:10b

The Bible tells us that God spoke and the waters under the heaven were gathered together into one place. God called these waters "seas." Sometimes we call them **oceans**.

Do you know how many oceans there are? There are four oceans—the Pacific Ocean, the Atlantic Ocean, the Indian Ocean, and the Arctic Ocean. *Find them on the map below and color them blue.*

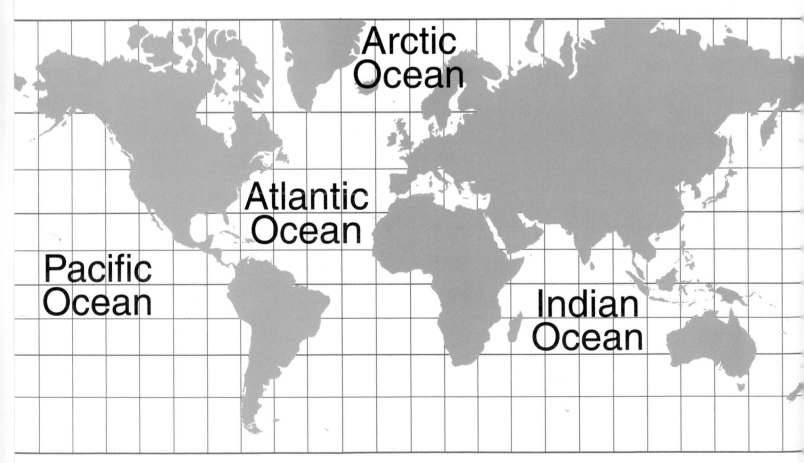

God Made Fresh Water

The water in the seas is **salty**. This means that sea water has salt in it. It is so salty that people and animals cannot drink it. So God made fresh water for them to drink. Fresh water does not have salt in it.

WHERE CAN YOU FIND FRESH WATER?

God made lakes and rivers with fresh water in them. Every living thing drinks from them. Where do lakes and rivers get their water? Every time it rains, fresh water fills them up again.

Rain is fresh water that helps to fill up lakes and rivers again.

25

God Created the Plants

Then God said, "Let the earth bring forth grass, the herb that yields seed, and the fruit tree that yields fruit according to its kind." Genesis 1:11a

On Day Three of creation, God made the plants. They grow in the soil. Why do plants need the soil? They get food and water from the soil. Without the soil, plants cannot live.

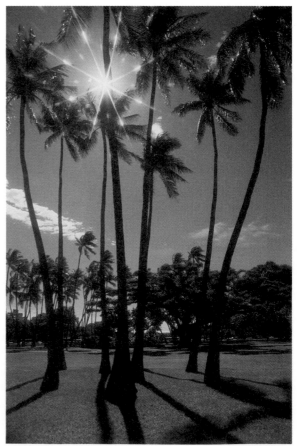

Some plants have soft stems like some flowers; others have hard stems like trees and bushes. What does the stem do? It holds up the plant. It is the part of the plant that holds the leaves, branches, flowers, and fruit.

Grass

God made grasses with soft stems. When grasses grow, they spread out and cover the ground. These plants live only for about six months, then they dry up and turn brown.

Grass plants make food you like to eat. Corn, oats, rice, and wheat are part of the grass family.

Animals also like to eat grass plants. Can you think of animals that like to eat corn and oats? Yes, cows and pigs like to eat corn, and horses like to eat oats.

Most grass plants are small, but bamboo is one kind of tall grass.

27

Flowers

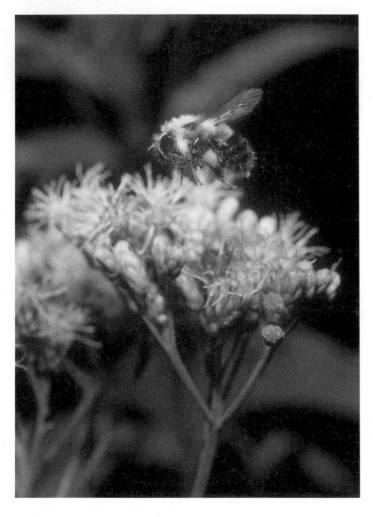

God made many plants with beautiful flowers. These flowers come in different colors. Bees like these colors and come to drink the sweet "juice" that the flowers make. Bees like to make honey from this "juice."

As a bee drinks the "juice" of the flower it picks up yellow dust on its legs. This yellow dust is called **pollen**. The center of the flower makes the yellow dust. Baby bees like to eat the pollen of flowers.

Activity

Hold up a rose (or any flower with a lot of petals) and guess how many petals are on it. Then count the rose petals and see if you were right. This is fun to play with the whole family.

Trees

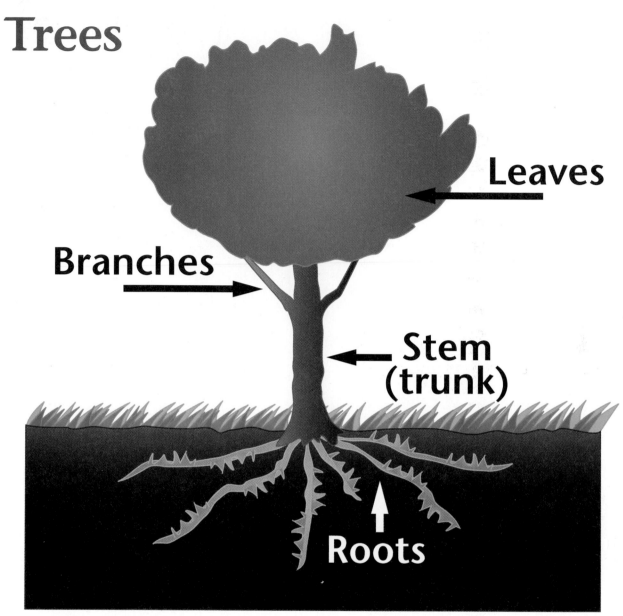

Leaves

Branches

Stem (trunk)

Roots

Trees are large plants with big stems and woody branches. They live many years and produce a lot of wood in their stems and branches. These plants have one tall stem made of wood.

God made these wonderful plants for us to enjoy and use in many different ways. Trees give us fruit to eat, wood to build, fresh air to breath, and many other helpful things.

Trees have roots, a stem (or trunk), branches, and leaves. Most trees also have flowers and fruit.

Bushes

God also made the bushes. They are plants that grow low to the ground like grass plants. But bushes have woody branches like trees. These branches grow up near the ground.

Different bushes have different kinds of leaves. Some leaves are smooth and shiny. Others are scaly like a cedar tree, and some are like the needles of pine trees.

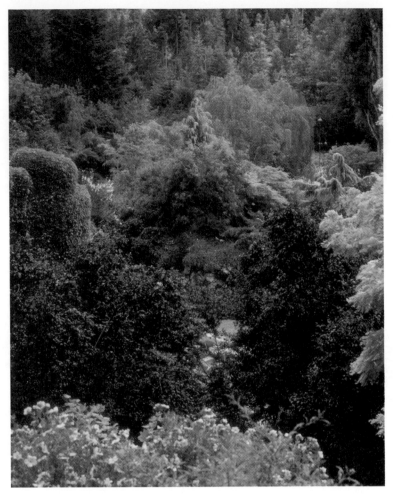

Draw green leaves on the bush.

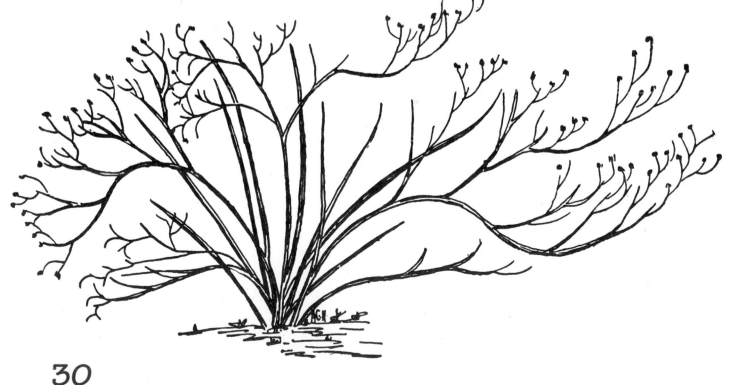

Leaves

God made most leaves flat and wide, but some trees and bushes have leaves that look like needles. Grasses have long leaves that are narrow (not wide). These are the three main kinds of leaves.

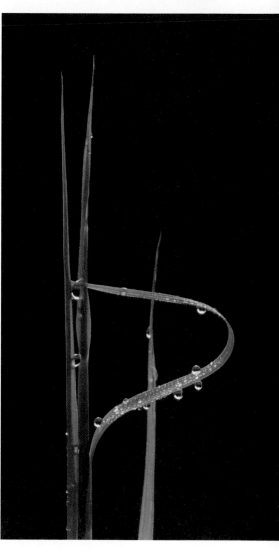

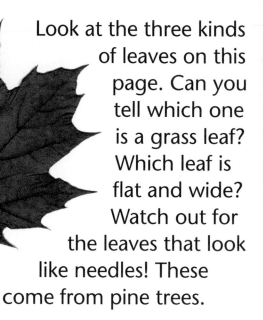

Look at the three kinds of leaves on this page. Can you tell which one is a grass leaf? Which leaf is flat and wide? Watch out for the leaves that look like needles! These come from pine trees.

Activity

Collect some leaves near your home. Place them under a blank sheet of paper. Then rub a crayon over the paper. What do you see? The small dark lines are called the **veins** of the leaf. Leaves take in food through these veins.

31

Looking Back

Questions

1. What did God divide on the third day of creation?
2. Why did God create the dry land?
3. What two things are found in soil?
4. Name the four oceans.
5. Why did God make fresh water?

Matching

grasses	yellow dust of a flower
trees	plants with hard stems
oceans	plants with soft stems
pollen	gathered waters or seas

Fill in the blank

1. Soil is good because it helps plants to _____.
2. _____ is made only of tiny bits of rock.
3. The water in the seas is _____.
4. _____ have roots, a stem (or trunk), branches, and leaves.
5. _____ are plants that grow low to the ground and have woody branches.

DAY 4
The Sun, Moon, and Stars

Then God said, "Let there be lights in the firmament of the heavens to divide the day from the night; and let them be for signs and seasons, and for days and years." Genesis 1:14

God Made the Sun

Then God made two great lights: the greater light to rule the day.... Genesis 1:16a

On Day Four of creation, God made the lights in the sky. Can you name a very big light that shines on the earth? If you said the sun, you are right. It is a huge ball of light that shines during the day.

WHY DID GOD MAKE THE SUN?

God made the sun so you can see. Without the sun, you cannot work or play. The sun also helps your skin to make **vitamin** D. This important vitamin helps your body build strong bones and teeth.

The sun also tells us what time it is during the day. When the sun rises in the morning, the day begins. When the sun is over your head, it is noon. When the sun goes down, the day is almost over.

Warning! DO NOT look directly at the sun. You may go blind.

Sunrise   **Noon**   **Sunset**

Activity

Buy two small plants that are the same. Put one plant in the sunlight; put the other plant in a closet. Be sure to water both of them if the dirt around them is dry.

After a few days, look at both plants. Which plant is growing? Why is this so? The sun helps plants to grow.

God Made the Moon

Then God made two great lights: ... the lesser light to rule the night. Genesis 1:16b

God made lights for the night sky. One of them is a large ball called the moon. The moon is made of rock; but when the sun shines on it, it looks like a bright "light" shining in the night.

You can see the moon when it is not cloudy outside. On a clear night, look at the moon. Sometimes it looks round like a dish. At other times it looks like half a dish. It can also look like a **crescent**.

 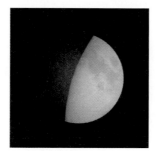 

IS THE MOON LIKE THE EARTH?

The moon is much smaller than the earth. The moon also does not have air or water; but the earth is filled with water and has lots of air around it. The surface of the moon only has rocks and dust on it. Earth's surface has water, rocks, soil, and living things on it.

Activity

Look at the moon every night for one month. You will see many of the "shapes" it makes. The moon is round like a ball, but the light from the sun shines on the moon differently each day.

Ask your teacher to make a one-month calendar on poster board. Then on each day of the month, draw the "shape" of the moon you see. How does the "shape" of the moon seem to change?

God Made the Stars

He made the stars also. Genesis 1:16c

God also made the stars. These are lights that twinkle in the night sky. They are huge balls of light like the sun, but they look very small to us on Earth. They look small because they are far away.

The Bible says, "[God] counts the number of the stars; He calls them all by name. Great is our Lord, and mighty in power; His understanding is infinite" (Psalms 147:4, 5; cf. Isaiah 40:26).

Activity

God put some of the stars into groups. Each group of stars is called a **constellation**. Get a book about constellations from the library. During the night, see if you can find some of them in the sky.

Signs and Seasons

The Bible tells us that God made the sun, moon, and stars as signs. What is a **sign**? A sign tells us to do something, like a traffic sign. For example, a stop sign tells us to stop.

The sun is a sign that tell us how long a day is. The moon is a sign that tells us about how long a month is. All the lights in the sky tell us how long a year is—they tell us about the four seasons.

A year is divided into four **seasons**. Can you name them? They are called winter, spring, summer, and fall. Each season is about three months long. God has a special purpose for each season.

Winter
**January
February
March**

Spring
**April
May
June**

Summer
**July
August
September**

Fall
**October
November
December**

Winter

God made the winter for all His creation to rest. Many animals sleep all during the winter. The trees, bushes, and small plants also rest. They are waiting for spring to come.

Winter is a time when it is cool or cold outside. Sometimes, God sends cold rain. Other times, He sends the snow to cover the earth. Why does God send the snow? The snow helps keep the cold, cold wind from hurting the plants that are resting.

During the winter months, it never snows in some places, but it is often cool or rainy. In some parts of the world, it may even be warm. Near the equator, it is always like the summertime!

Color the picture.

Spring

Spring comes after the cold winter season. The sun shines longer, and the days become warmer. Spring is when the earth comes alive. God sends rain to help all the plants to grow.

Activity

Spring is the time to plant flowers or a small tree. If you have a garden, help your mom or dad plant some vegetables. If it is cold outside, start a few plants in clay pots inside. Watch them grow.

Summer

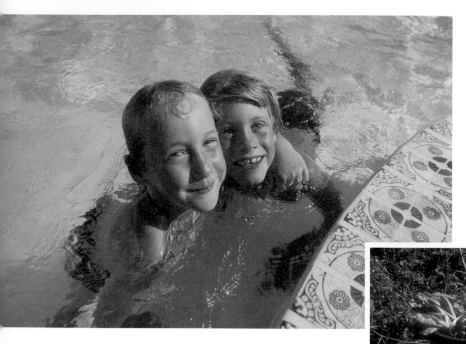

The summer comes after the spring season. The sun shines a lot on the earth and warms it up. It is a time to enjoy God's beautiful outdoors. What do you like to do during the summer?

WHY DID GOD MAKE THE SUMMER?

The summer is an important time of the year. It brings lots of sunshine which helps plants to grow fast. These plants make fruit and other good things for us to eat. Without the summer sun, these plants would not grow and we would have no food to eat.

Fall

Fall is the season that comes after summer. This is the time when many leaves change their color and fall off the trees. Some leaves turn dark brown or bright yellow; others turn deep red or orange.

If you live in a part of the world where the leaves fall off the trees, maybe you can help **rake** them. Do you know what "rake" means? It means to gather together. After you have raked the leaves in a pile, it can be a lot of fun playing and jumping in the leaves.

Fall is also the time when fruit and vegetables **ripen**. This means they are ready to eat. There is so much food that we cannot eat all of it. During the fall, many people store food for the wintertime.

Activity

Collect some leaves near your home. Dry them by putting them between two sheets of wax paper. Place a heavy book on them for two or three days. Then glue the leaves on a piece of paper.

Looking Back

Questions

1. What did God create on the fourth day of creation?

2. Why did God create the sun?

3. Is it safe to look directly at the sun? Why?

4. Does the moon have air and water?

5. What is a constellation?

Matching

moon   huge ball of light

stars   large ball of rock

sun   huge balls of light

Fill in the blank

1. God made the sun, moon, and stars as _____.

2. A year is divided into four _____.

3. God made the winter for all His creation to _____.

4. In spring, God sends _____ to help the plants grow.

5. Fall is the time when fruit and vegetables _____.

Name the four seasons.

_____   _____

_____   _____

DAY 5
The Fish and Birds

Then God said, "Let the waters abound with an abundance of living creatures, and let birds fly above the earth across the face of the firmament of the heavens."

Genesis 1:20

God Created Living Things

On Day Five of creation, God made something wonderful. He created living creatures. God made great sea creatures, smaller sea creatures, and winged birds.

Look at these pictures of sea creatures and birds. Do you know the names of any of them? Match the names to the correct picture. If you do not know their names, ask your teacher to help you.

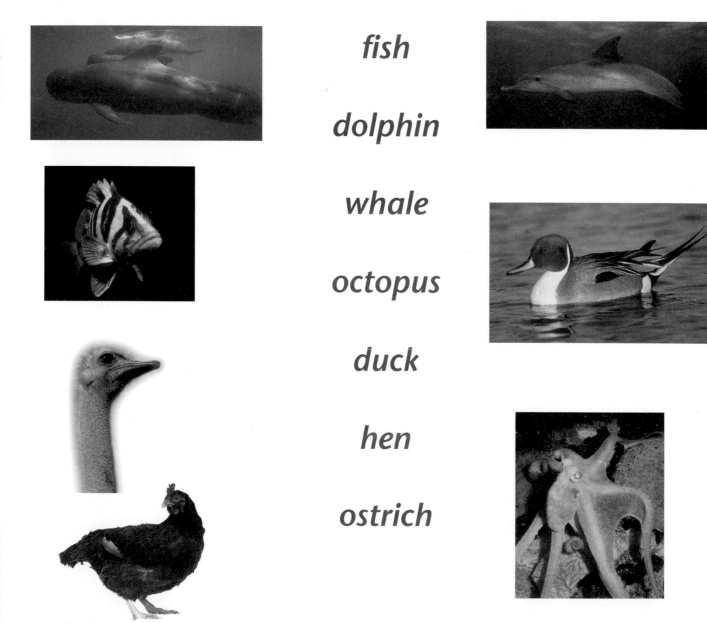

fish

dolphin

whale

octopus

duck

hen

ostrich

The Huge Whale

Did you know that whales are the largest animals in the world? Some whales have "teeth" that hang down from the top of their mouths and look like combs. As they drink, the whales eat large shrimplike sea creatures which get caught in their "teeth."

The largest animal in the world is the blue whale. It is bigger than the biggest dinosaur that ever lived. The blue whale grows to 100 feet long and weighs up to 150 tons! The blue whale makes very loud sounds when it "talks."

Color the blue whale.

The Dashing Dolphin

The dolphin is like a small whale. It is very smart and likes to play. God made the dolphin with a hole in the top of its head. This hole is called a **spout**. It uses its spout to breathe.

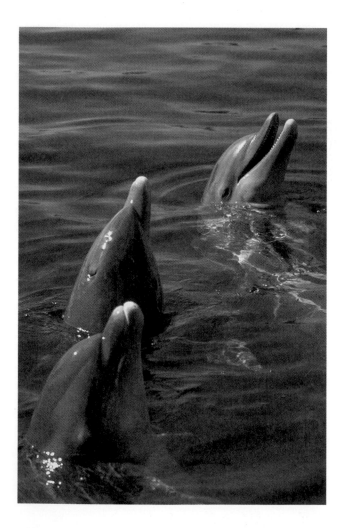

The bottle-nosed dolphin looks like it is always smiling. It is very friendly with people. This dolphin enjoys following ships in the ocean. It jumps out of the water as the ships move.

God Made *the Fish*

Did you ever eat fish for dinner? Fish taste good. God made fish for us to eat. They live in the water, where they like to swim. God made fish to live their whole lives in the water.

God made fish with skeletons. Do you know what a **skeleton** is? It is the part of an animal that holds up its body. The skeleton also protects the fish's inner parts. Most fish have skeletons made of bone.

Gills and Fins

Do you know how fish breathe? They breathe while they swim in the water. First they drink some water. After the fish closes its mouth, the water goes through its **gills** and out of its body.

Gill Cover

Gills

How do gills help a fish breathe? A fish's gills collect tiny bubbles of air from the water. After the water goes out of its body, the fish uses the tiny bubbles of air to breathe.

A fish also has special "hands" and "feet" for swimming. These are called **fins**. A fish swims in the water by moving its fins back and forth. Fish have fins that come in different shapes and sizes.

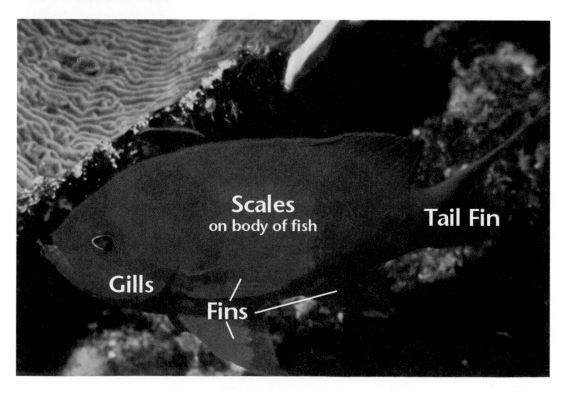

Scales
on body of fish

Tail Fin

Gills

Fins

Small Sea Creatures

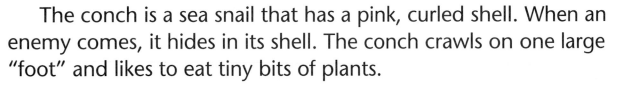

God created many small sea creatures that live in the water. You may not have heard of them. Some of them have shells, and others do not have any bones. None of them have backbones.

The conch is a sea snail that has a pink, curled shell. When an enemy comes, it hides in its shell. The conch crawls on one large "foot" and likes to eat tiny bits of plants.

The starfish is another small sea creature that looks like a funny-looking rock. Do you know how it got its name? Yes, the starfish looks like a star. It has five "arms" that look like the points of a star.

The octopus is a sea creature that does not have a shell. It has a very soft body with eight "legs."

Each "leg" has two rows of **suckers** that look like little suction cups. The octopus uses them to move. An octopus can be as short as 2 inches or as long as 18 feet!

49

God Made the Birds

Then God said, "... and let birds fly above the earth across the face of the firmament of the heavens." Genesis 1:20b.

Macaw

On Day Five, God also created birds. He made them to fly fast and far. Have you ever watched birds fly? Flying helps them to find food and to quickly get away from their enemies.

Did you know that birds have wings? All birds have wings, but not all birds can fly. Some birds like the ostrich, penguin, and kiwi bird can only walk or run on the ground. Most birds can fly, however.

Kiwi bird

Most birds fly close to the ground. Some can fly high in the sky. A few birds can even fly over mountains! The falcon is a bird that can fly high and fast. It can fly up to 200 miles per hour!

Peregrine Falcon

How Did God Make Birds?

God made most birds with small bodies that are light. They also have skeletons made of strong bones. Do you remember what a **skeleton** is? It is the part of an animal that holds up its body.

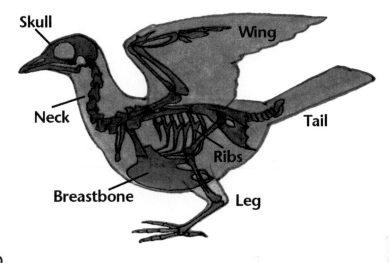

Skull

Neck

Breastbone

Ribs

Wing

Tail

Leg

Kestral

God gave each bird two important gifts—feathers and wings. Other animals do not have these gifts. A bird's feathers are attached to its wings. Feathers and wings help the bird to fly.

God gave special kinds of wings to each bird. The wings of an eagle help it to fly high and far. The wings of a sparrow help it to fly fast in the air. The wings of a penguin help it to swim.

Swallow

Penguins

51

The Quacking Duck

God made the duck with special feet. It spends a lot of time in the water, so God gave the duck webbed feet. Why do you think God gave them webbed feet? Webbed feet help the duck to swim.

The duck also has special feathers. The duck keeps its feathers straight and clean with its beak. It uses its beak to oil its feathers, too. This keeps water off its body and helps it to float.

Name the parts of the duck in the picture below.

The Big Ostrich

The ostrich is the largest living bird in the world. God first put this bird in Africa. Now, however, the ostrich lives in many parts of the world. A baby ostrich comes from the largest egg in the world. This egg can be 6 inches long and weigh up to 3 pounds!

An ostrich can grow up to 8 feet tall and weigh over 300 pounds! Most birds have four toes, but the ostrich is the only bird that has two toes. God made the ostrich with a small head, long neck, and powerful legs. Its legs help it to run up to 40 miles per hour.

Looking Back

Questions

1. What did God create on Day Five of creation?
2. What is the largest animal in the world?
3. What is the hole on the top of a dolphin's head called?
4. What two important gifts did God give to birds?

Matching

gills   help octopuses move

fins   help fish swim

suckers   help fish breathe

Fill in the blank

1. The octopus has a very soft body with _____ legs.

2. The _____ looks like a star with five points.

3. The _____ is the part of an animal that holds up its body.

4. The duck has _____ feet for swimming.

5. The _____ is the largest bird in the world.

DAY 6
The Land Animals and Man

Then God said, "Let the earth bring forth the living creature according to its kind: cattle and creeping thing and beast of the earth, each according to its kind"; and it was so.
Genesis 1:24

Then God said, "Let us make man in Our image, according to Our likeness...."
Genesis 1:26a

Beasts Of The Earth

On Day Six of creation, the Bible tells us that God made three groups of animals. He made the beasts of the earth, cattle, and creeping things. The largest animals belong to the group called the beasts of the earth. What are some of these large animals called?

Matching

Draw a line from the animal to the group to which it belongs.

BEASTS OF THE EARTH

CATTLE

CREEPING THINGS

God made the elephants, lions, tigers, bears, and more. These wild animals walk freely over the world. God also made the dinosaurs. God made all of these beasts of the earth in one day!

The Huge Dinosaur

The largest beasts God made no longer live on the earth. They probably died either during the Great Flood or shortly after it. Do you know what they are called? They are called dinosaurs.

Not all dinosaurs were huge. The Compsognathus is the smallest known dinosaur. It was as small as a chicken. Some people think that there may still be dinosaurs that live deep in the ocean.

The largest dinosaur God made was the brachiosaur. It was as tall as a seven-story building and weighed as much as ten elephants! God gave it a long neck to eat the leaves high on the trees.

The Big Elephant

What animal has big ears and a long nose? Yes, an elephant. The African elephant is the largest land animal in the world. It grows to 13 feet tall and weighs as much as four cars put together!

God gave the elephant ears that look like fans. Why did He give it big ears? When the elephant **flaps** its ears, it moves air around its body. This is how an elephant keeps cool in the hot sun.

God also gave the elephant a big nose called a **trunk**. Its trunk is about 6 feet long! The elephant uses its trunk to eat. It pulls up bunches of tall grass and breaks off leaves from trees. Then the elephant sticks the food in its mouth. It drinks with its trunk, too.

The Zippy Zebra

What animal looks like a horse and has black and white stripes all over its body? If you said the zebra, you are right. This "striped horse" grows to be about 8 feet tall!

God made the zebra to run very fast. Its strong legs help it run away from lions which try to eat it for lunch! The zebra does not like to eat other animals. It only eats grass and leaves.

Connect the dots and color the picture. What do you see?

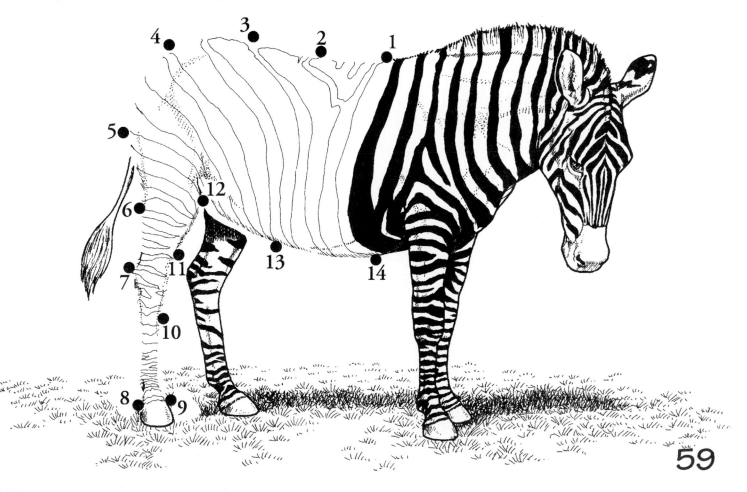

The Helpful Horse

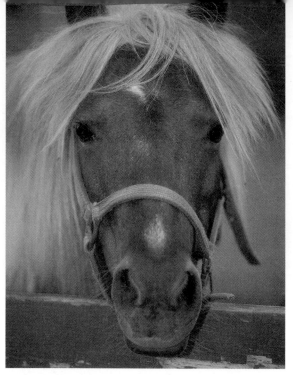

Do you like horses? They are one of the most beautiful animals that God has made. It is fun to ride on their backs. This is called horseback riding. God made horses very strong and fast.

The horse can help people in many ways. Do you know how the horse helps people? It can help people travel. It can also carry heavy loads and pull wagons.

Years ago, horses helped farmers plow their fields. They also helped soldiers fight in many wars. In 1860, horses even helped men to deliver the mail. They would carry the mail from the state of Missouri all the way to California.

The Fuzzy Bear

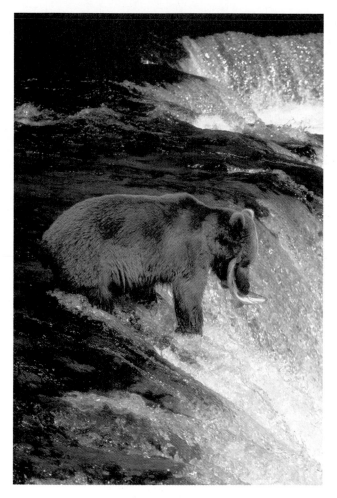

Do you have a fuzzy stuffed bear? It is called a "teddy bear." It is named after a president of the United States. His name was Teddy Roosevelt. He loved the outdoors and was a great bear hunter.

The largest bear in the world is the Alaskan brown bear. It lives on Kodiak Island in Alaska. Sometimes it is called a Kodiak bear. It has a large head, long nose, and a short tail. Instead of feet, it has paws; each paw has five toes; and each toe has one claw on it.

The Cuddly Cat

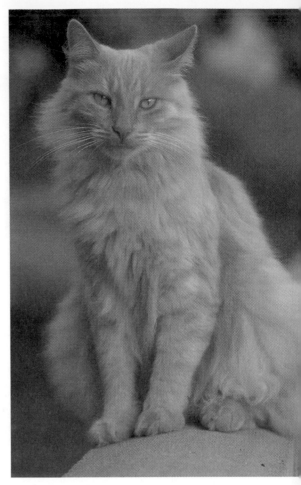

Do you have a pet cat? What is its name? A pet cat usually likes to be alone, but it can be playful and loving. If you are gentle and kind with your pet, you can teach it to do many things. A pet cat may live to be more than twenty years old.

God made cats with sharp teeth and long whiskers. God also gave them special eyes which help them hunt for food. Their feet are padded so they can walk quietly and catch their **prey**. Do you know what "prey" is? It is an animal that is hunted for food.

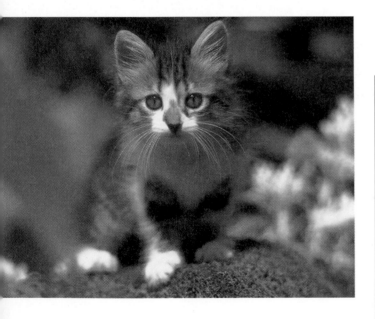

Draw a picture of a cat.

The Mighty Tiger

God made little pet cats and big jungle cats, too. The tiger is the largest and strongest cat in the world. It likes to live in the forests of Asia. Big cats such as the tiger also like to be alone.

During the day, it hides among the tall grasses near the water. Sometimes it likes to go swimming. At night, the tiger hunts alone. It eats deer, monkeys, cows, fish, and other animals.

The tiger stands only 4 feet tall, but it is 9 feet long! Its tail alone is 3 feet long. The tiger is striped like the zebra, but its stripes are reddish-orange and black. God made them fast and strong.

The Friendly Dog

Do you have a pet dog? What is its name? God made your pet dog with a special nose and ears. It cannot see colors, but it uses its nose and ears to find many things. A pet dog can also protect you when you are in danger. A pet dog can be a good friend.

Dogs are very smart. They have helped people for many years. Dogs like to do tricks and can learn to obey commands. They can hunt animals, herd sheep, and guard homes.

The Funny Monkey

Monkeys can be tall or short, big or small. Some weigh only two ounces; others weigh as much as 100 pounds, like the baboon. All monkeys have long tails. They use their tails like another hand.

Some monkeys may hurt people; but most monkeys can learn to be obedient, if they are caught when they are young.

A few kinds of monkeys make wonderful pets. These pets are very smart and can do things to make people laugh.

Color the baboons.

65

The Hopping Kangaroo

God made an animal with a "pocket" in front of its stomach. This animal has powerful back legs and feet on which it hops and leaps; it also has a strong tail to keep its balance. Do you know the name of this animal? It is the kangaroo. It has soft and woolly fur.

What do you think the kangaroo keeps in its "pocket"? Yes, it keeps its baby there. A baby red kangaroo stays in its mother's "pocket" for as long as 8 months. A baby kangaroo needs to stay in its mother's "pocket" because it is born blind and has no hair.

The Eager Beaver

God made the beaver in a special way. He gave it a wide, flat tail which is about one foot long. Its tail helps the beaver to swim in the water. The beaver also uses its tail to warn its family when danger is near; it slaps its tail in the water to sound an alarm.

God also gave the beaver sharp teeth. It uses its teeth to cut down trees. It cuts them into pieces to build a **dam**. Do you know what a dam is? It is something that holds back water from flowing in a river. The dam helps to keep the water deep around the beaver's house.

The beaver also uses wood from trees to build its house. Wood and mud help to make the beaver's house strong and warm for the winter. To get inside, the beaver swims underwater to a hole in the bottom of its house; then it goes up into its warm, dry home.

The Gentle Rabbit

Have you ever held a rabbit? It is soft and very gentle. God gave the rabbit a short tail, long fuzzy ears, and a cute nose. A rabbit makes a wonderful pet, but it takes a lot of work to care for it. You have to give it food and water every day and keep its cage clean.

How does a mother rabbit care for her babies? She digs a hole in the ground and builds a nest; the mother uses leaves and some of her own fur. She builds her nest near a grassy field for food.

A mother rabbit can have babies five or more times each year.

Looking Back

Questions

1. How big was the brachiosaur?
2. How does an elephant keep cool?
3. What animal looks like a horse and has black and white stripes?
4. How does the horse help people?
5. What is the largest bear in the world?

Matching

"pocket"	elephant's nose
prey	holds back water from flowing in a river
dam	an animal that is hunted for food
trunk	where a kangaroo keeps its baby

Fill in the blanks

1. A pet _____ may live to be more than twenty years old.
2. A _____ builds its house in deep water.
3. The _____ is the largest cat in the world.
4. A _____ can hunt animals, herd sheep, and guard homes.
5. A _____ has a long tail and uses it like another hand.

Cattle

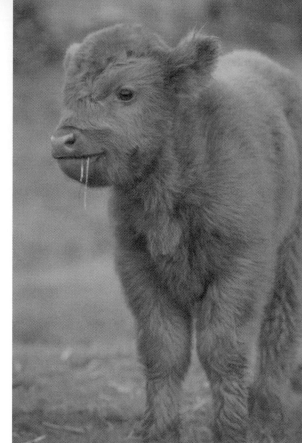

On Day Six, God created a second group of animals called "cattle." All cattle grow horns or antlers and have four legs. This group includes many farm animals. Can you name some of them? Cows, sheep, and goats are three kinds of farm animals.

All cattle chew their **cud**. Do you know what "cud" is? It is the grass and plants that cattle have eaten.

Cattle quickly eat their food and put it in their stomach. After the food becomes soft, they chew their cud again. Now it is ready for them to use as food.

70

The Useful Cow

God created the cow to help people in many ways. Some cows are raised for their milk. Do you like to drink milk? It is filled with good things for you. It is sometimes called the "perfect" food.

Why is milk so good for you? It gives you things (proteins, fats, minerals, and vitamins) which help build strong, healthy bones and teeth. Milk also gives you energy to run and play.

Cows are also raised for their meat. This meat is called **beef**. Do you eat food made with beef? Hamburgers, meat balls, and sometimes hot dogs are made with cow's meat.

71

Sheep and Goats

Sheep are fuzzy animals found all over the world. Most sheep are raised for their wool and meat. In some places, skins of sheep are sold as fur. In other places, cheese is made from the milk of sheep.

Goats are a lot like sheep, but their hair is different. Their hair is made into beautiful clothing. Goats are mostly raised for their milk and meat. They like to eat grass, shrubs, leaves, and twigs.

In the pictures below, circle the sheep and put an "X" on the goats.

The Graceful Deer

Deer are found all over the world. Deer, including moose and elk, are the only animals that grow antlers. Do you know what

antlers are? They are the horns on top of a deer's head. They look like tree branches and are made of solid bone. Deer grow new antlers every spring.

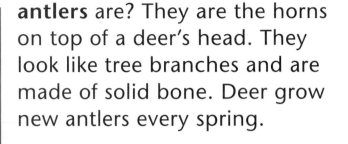

Deer live mostly in the woods, but some live in grasslands. They like to eat grass, bushes, twigs, bark,

and **shoots** (young tree plants or branches). A baby deer is called a **fawn**, and its coat is covered with white spots. A fawn stays with its mother for about a year.

Looking Back

Questions

1. What do all cattle have?
2. What are three kinds of farm animals?
3. What two foods come from cows?
4. What animals are a lot like sheep?
5. What is the only group of animals that grow antlers?

Matching

beef   horns of deer

fawn   baby deer

antlers   cow's meat

Fill in the blank

1. All cattle chew their _____.
2. _____ gives you energy to run and play.
3. Most _____ are raised for their wool and meat.
4. _____ like to eat grass, shrubs, leaves, and twigs.
5. Deer like to eat grass, bushes, twigs, bark, and _____.

Creeping Things

On Day Six, God created creeping things. These are the smallest animals in the world. Some are so small that they are hard to see. Others are so tiny that a special tool is needed to see them. This tool is called a **microscope**.

Creeping things include creatures like the skunk, mouse, snake, turtle, frog, grasshopper, and butterfly. God made so many of these little creatures that all of them cannot be put in this book!

Activity

If you have a microscope, look at the small creatures that live in water. Get some water from a mud puddle, water hole, or pond. Put a drop of this water under the microscope. What do you see moving? These are tiny creatures that God has made.

If you do not have a microscope, you can use a magnifying glass. Take a special trip to a park or forest and look at small creatures under rocks or dead branches. Ants are always fun to watch as they work. Also look for little creatures in a pond or mud puddle.

The Stinky Skunk

What animal has black fur and two white stripes down its back? It is the skunk. Do you know how the skunk protects itself? When an enemy comes near, the skunk sprays it with **musk**. The musk smells very bad and burns the face, so the enemy runs away fast.

Color the spotted skunk. It is black with white spots.

The skunk grows to be about two feet long and has a long bushy tail. It lives in a hole in the ground with other skunks. At night, it looks for food. It likes to eat plants and small animals. Since the skunk is gentle and playful, some people like to keep it as a pet!

The Little Mouse

The mouse is found all over the world. It has a small body, pointed nose, ears that stand up, and a tail with very little hair. A mouse likes to bite down on things like wood, over and over again.

Wild mice carry **diseases**. Do you know what a disease is? It is something that makes people very sick. Sometimes wild mice pass these diseases on to people. You should stay away from wild mice!

Some people like to keep a mouse as a pet. If you want a pet mouse, you should get a healthy one from a pet shop. You need to take care of your pet mouse by giving it food and water.

The Crafty Snake

A snake is a creature without legs. Since it does not have legs, how does the snake move? It wiggles its body back and forth; this helps it to move forward. Can you wiggle back and forth like a snake?

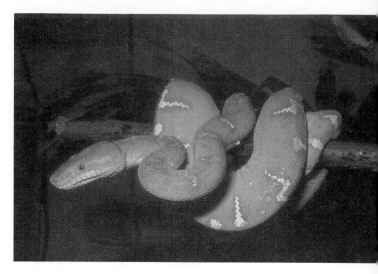

Most snakes are small, but some grow to be 30 feet long! God gave all of them special eyelids. Their eyelids are always "closed"! If you close your eyelids, you cannot see; but snakes can see right through their eyelids. How do they see? Their eyelids are clear.

Snakes are very helpful to people. They eat a lot of small animals that may harm people or destroy crops that farmers grow. Snakes eat fish, frogs, mice, birds, and other small creatures.

The Humble Turtle

God made the turtle with a "house" on its back. Do you know what its "house" is called? It is called a **shell**. Its shell protects the turtle from its enemies. All it has to do is pull in its head, legs, and tail, and it is safe! The turtle carries its shell everywhere it goes.

Some turtles can be held in your hand, but some grow to be 8 feet long and weigh as much as a car! All turtles do not have teeth. How can they eat without teeth? God gave them a mouth with sharp edges on it. These sharp edges help the turtle chew its food.

Color the turtle above.

The Lively Frog

God made a special animal that is born in the water and lives on the land after it grows up. Do you know what its name is? It is the frog. It has a big head, webbed feet, and large back legs. The frog uses its back legs to jump, hop, swim, dig tunnels, and climb.

Most frogs lay eggs in water. After the eggs hatch, the baby frogs start to swim like fish. Do you know what baby frogs are called? They are called **tadpoles**. They look more like fish than frogs!

A tadpole breathes through **gills**. Do you remember what gills do? They take tiny air bubbles out of the water for sea creatures to breathe. As a baby frog grows, it forms legs and looks more like a frog. When it is fully grown, the frog begins to live on land.

The Amazing Grasshopper

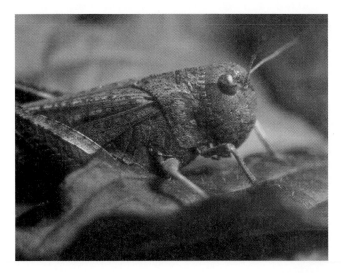

The grasshopper is an **insect**. Do you know what an insect is? An insect is a small creature with three body parts and six legs. A grasshopper is an insect that is green or brown.

God gave the grasshopper large back legs for leaping and wings for flying. It may grow to over four inches long. The grasshopper likes to eat plants. A few kinds may ruin the farmer's crop.

God made the grasshopper with two sets of eyes! Its three simple eyes help it notice light, and its two big eyes help it see.

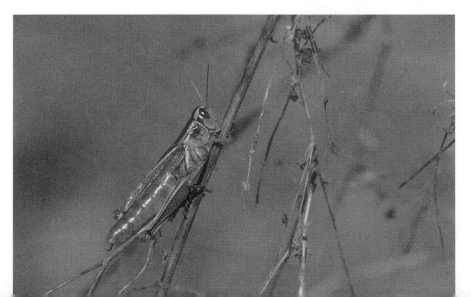

Each big eye has many little "cameras" that help it see. It does not need to turn its head to see. It can look everywhere at the same time!

81

The Beautiful Butterfly

God made many, many kinds of pretty butterflies. They are found all over the world. Butterflies have wings that are filled with bright, beautiful colors. They also have a special kind of nose that looks like a straw. They use their noses to drink "juice" from flowers.

A butterfly changes three times as it grows up.

1. First, a small egg is laid on the leaf of a plant.

2. After a while, a caterpillar hatches from the egg and feeds on plants.

3. Next, the caterpillar looses its skin and makes a special covering around its body.

4. Then, when the time is right, a beautiful butterfly breaks out of the covering and flies away.

Looking Back

Questions

1. How does the skunk protect itself?
2. What animal likes to bite down, over and over again?
3. How does a snake move?
4. What protects the turtle from its enemies?
5. How does the frog use its back legs?

Matching

disease	tool to see tiny creatures
microscope	help tadpoles breathe
gills	something that makes people sick

Fill in the blank

1. God gave snakes clear eyelids that are always _____.
2. After baby frogs grow up, they live on _____.
3. An _____ is a small creature with three body parts and six legs.
4. God made the grasshopper with two sets of _____.
5. A _____ changes three times as it grows up.

Man

On Day Six, God also made the first man and woman. Do you know their names? Adam and Eve were the first people on Earth. God made them in a special way. He made them like Himself.

The Bible says, "God created man in His own image" (Genesis 1:27a). This means God gave everyone a spirit (Genesis 2:7). Each person was created to know God and worship Him in spirit and truth.

Activity

Draw a picture of your mom and dad in the picture frame below. If you have a photo of your parents, or of your whole family, you may want to glue it in the frame instead. Thank God for your family.

Five Gifts from God

God made each person in a special way. He gave most people five gifts to help them live on Earth. God gave us eyes to see, ears to hear, a nose to smell, a tongue to taste, and skin to feel. These five gifts show us that God is wise. Praise Him for these good gifts.

Pupil—Lens

The Eye

The eye is a wonderful gift from God. It helps you to see many things. God made the eye in the shape of a ball. The eye has an opening in the front that lets in the light. This opening is called the **pupil**. It looks like a black dot.

After light enters the pupil, the light reaches the back of the eye. Then the back of the eye changes what you see into "messages" that are sent to the brain. Now you are able to see.

Activity

Look around the room. What do you see? Name five things you can see with your eyes. Can you see different colors? Name as many colors as you can see. How many shapes do you see? Name things that look like a circle or square, a ball or box.

85

The Ear

God gave you another gift—the ear. It helps you to hear sounds. God made the outside of the ear to catch sounds, like a baseball mitt helps you catch a ball. Then the ear changes the sounds to little "messages" that are sent to your brain so you can hear.

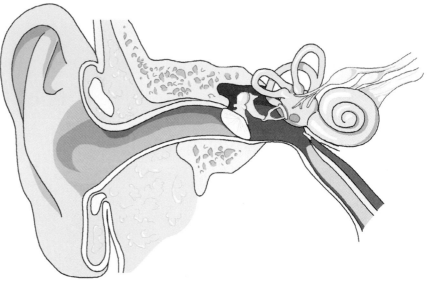

Be careful not to put anything in your ears that is small. It may hurt your ears and you will not be able to hear. Also do not make loud noises near your ears; this could harm your ears as well.

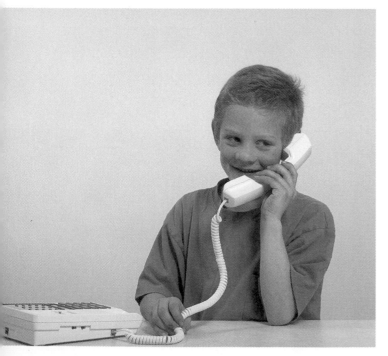

Activity

Sit quietly and listen. What do you hear? Name five things you can hear with your ears. Then make some sounds with a musical instrument or with one of your toys. Does it make a loud or soft sound? Is it nice to listen to the "music" you make?

The Nose

Another gift God gave to you is the nose. It helps you to smell many good things. You can smell the cookies your mother is baking. You can smell the flowers in your yard. Your nose helps you to smell food, flowers, and many other wonderful things.

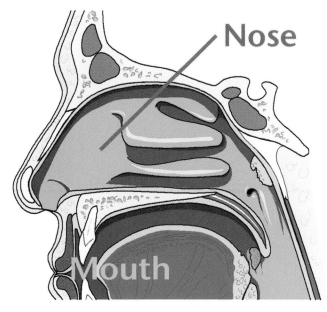

Your nose helps you to breathe too. You breathe mostly through your nose, but you can also breathe through your mouth. Close your mouth. Can you breathe? Yes, you can breathe when your mouth is closed. God made your nose in a special way.

Activity

Walk around your house. What do smell? Name five things you can smell with your

nose. Try smelling different kinds of food.

If you go outside, you can smell flowers, newly mowed grass, and pine trees. You can even smell if the air is fresh or not.

The Tongue

The tongue is a gift from God that you can enjoy. It tells you what food tastes like. It tells you if food is sweet, salty, sour, or bitter. What do you like to taste that is sweet? What do you like to taste that is salty? The tongue helps us to enjoy many kinds of food.

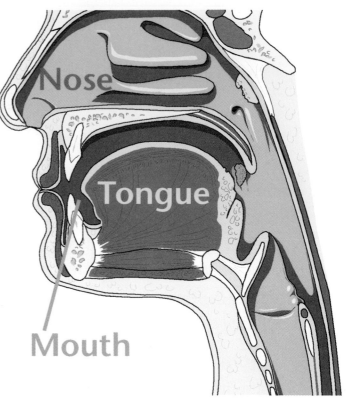

Nose

Tongue

Mouth

Sour

God also made the tongue to help you talk. It helps you make the sounds of letters in the **alphabet**. How many letters of the alphabet are made by using the tongue? Yes, all of them are made with it. God was very wise to give people the gift of the tongue.

Sweet

88

The **Skin**

The skin is one of God's most wonderful gifts. It covers all of your body. The skin helps you to feel many things. The tips of your fingers can tell you if something is smooth like glass. If you touch your father's beard, your fingers tell you that it is rough.

Your skin can also tell you if something is hard or soft. Your fingertips tell you that a table is hard and that cotton is soft. Your skin can also tell you if something is cold or hot, warm or cool. Can you name something that is cold or hot? Warm or cool?

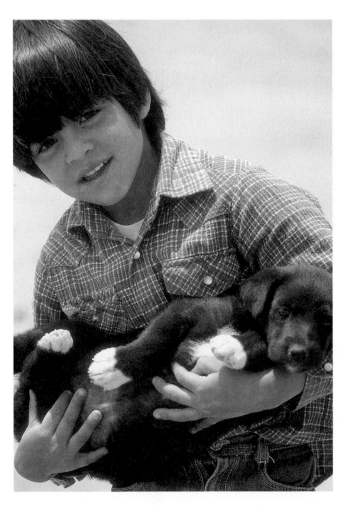

Activity

Find different things around the house that are rough or smooth, hard or soft, cold or hot, warm or cool. Be careful not to touch things that are too hot. You may burn your fingers!

Looking Back

Questions

1. Who did God create on Day Six?
2. Name five gifts God gave to people.
3. In what shape did God make the eye?
4. How does the nose help people?
5. How does the tongue help people?

Fill in the blank

1. The Bible says, "God created _____ in His own image."

2. God made the outside of the _____ to catch sounds.

3. The opening in the front of the eye is called the _____.

4. God made the _____ to help you to talk.

5. The _____ helps you to feel many things.

DAY 7
God Rested

And on the seventh day God ended His work which He had done, and He rested on the seventh day from all His work which He had done.
Genesis 2:2

Worshiping God

God created everything in six days, and on Day Seven, God rested. His example teaches us to work for six days, and on the seventh day, we should rest from our work. God made the Sabbath for rest.

Every Sabbath, you should rest from your work and worship God. You should take time to pray to the great Creator. Thank Him for all the things He has made. Thank Him for making you. Also thank God for your family and friends.

Caring for God's Creation

You have studied about God's creation. God wants you to care for all that He has made. One way you can help is not to **litter**. Do you know what litter is? It is trash that some people throw on the ground. If you see litter, you can pick it up and put it in a trash can.

Activity

Ask your mom or dad to take you to a nearby park, or to your church, so you can pick up trash from the ground. Remember to bring a plastic bag and to wear a pair of gloves as you clean up God's creation. DO NOT pick up sharp objects or rotten things. Ask your parents for help if you are unsure of what to pick up.